NEGOTIATION

NEGOTIATION

BRIAN TRACY

AMACOM AMERICAN MANAGEMENT ASSOCIATION
New York · Atlanta · Brussels · Chicago · Mexico City
San Francisco · Shanghai · Tokyo · Toronto · Washington, D.C.

Bulk discounts available. For details visit:
www.amacombooks.org/go/specialsales
Or contact special sales:
Phone: 800-250-5308 / E-mail: specialsls@amanet.org
View all the AMACOM titles at: www.amacombooks.org

This publication is designed to provide accurate and authoritative information in regard to the subject matter covered. It is sold with the understanding that the publisher is not engaged in rendering legal, accounting, or other professional service. If legal advice or other expert assistance is required, the services of a competent professional person should be sought.

Library of Congress Cataloging-in-Publication Data

Tracy, Brian.
Negotiation / Brian Tracy.
    pages cm
Includes index.
ISBN 978-0-8144-3318-8 — ISBN 0-8144-3318-9 1. Negotiation in business.
I. Title.
HD58.6.T73 2013
658.4'052—dc23

                                                                    2013010064

About AMA

American Management Association (www.amanet.org) is a world leader in talent development, advancing the skills of individuals to drive business success. Our mission is to support the goals of individuals and organizations through a complete range of products and services, including classroom and virtual seminars, webcasts, webinars, podcasts, conferences, corporate and government solutions, business books, and research. AMA's approach to improving performance combines experiential learning—learning through doing—with opportunities for ongoing professional growth at every step of one's career journey.

Printing number
10 9 8 7 6 5 4 3 2 1

CONTENTS

Introduction

YOUR SUCCESS IN business and in life will be determined by your ability to negotiate in your best interests in every situation. Negotiating is a key skill that affects everything you do or say, and almost all of your interactions, both personal and in business. If you cannot negotiate well on your best behalf, then you automatically become the victim of people who are better negotiators than you. You will always achieve a better income, or get a better deal, if you are good at negotiating.

Life may be viewed as one long, extended negotiating session, from the cradle to the grave. Negotiation never stops. It is a major part of the business of living and communicating with others. It is the way that individuals with differing values and interests find constructive ways to live and work together in harmony. Your ability to negotiate successfully is essential to your success in all your interactions with other people.

Negotiating has been going on since the beginning of civilization because humans have always had an interest in improving their relative position in life. Everyone wants to achieve more of those things that are good—happiness, wealth, position, love, security, status, prestige, and success. And people want to achieve their goals in ways that are faster and easier, and at the lowest possible cost of time and money. Every one of us is in a form of competition with many other people who also want to achieve the same goals, results, and outcomes.

It is by compromising, trading, and negotiating that we balance conflicting and competing wants and needs to ensure that we achieve the best possible outcome for ourselves.

Value Is Subjective

The price or value of anything is always and only determined by the level of demand or desire for that good. The value is determined by what a particular individual, at a particular time, under a particular set of circumstances, considers something to be worth.

Since this type of value judgment is always *subjective*, there is never a right and final price or set of terms that can be decided in advance. The prices that people are willing to pay or accept always depend on the individuals involved and their relative scale of needs at the time of the transaction. Subjective evaluations are what create the desire to exchange goods, services, money, and other things. In every voluntary trade or transaction, the parties involved will only agree with the prices and terms if they believe they will be *better off* afterward than if they had not entered into the negotiation or transaction at all. As they say, "It's differences of opinion that make a horse race."

Practical Strategies and Methods

Over the years, I have negotiated many millions of dollars' worth of contracts for residential, commercial, and industrial real estate, including shopping centers, office buildings, and land development. I have negotiated the importation and distribution of more than $25 million worth of automobiles, plus contracts for printing, consulting, training, advertising, conventions and meetings, and sales of thousands of items worth millions of dollars.

The ideas in this book are therefore based on extensive experience, both good and bad, supplemented by years of study into the art and science of negotiating. You are about to learn a series of the most important strategies and tactics ever discovered in the field of negotiating.

Each of these ideas is practical, proven, and applicable immediately. They work, and they'll enable you to get a better deal in almost every situation. I have taught these skills to hundreds of thousands of businesspeople worldwide, and the positive results that they have achieved in negotiating have been life-changing. If you systematically apply even a small part of what you are about to learn, you can bring about a major improvement in the quality and quantity of your results.

Negotiating Is Learnable

Even little children negotiate. They know that little hugs and affection are the currency with which they negotiate with their parents and relatives. Negotiating (or not negotiating), compromising (or refusing to compromise), and working to reconcile conflicting interests—these activities are an essential part of human life. Your ability to negotiate well can make an extraordinary difference in your financial life, your career, your relationships, and almost everything you get or give in the course of daily life.

Fortunately, negotiating is a skill, and all skills are learnable. Everyone who is an excellent negotiator today was once a poor negotiator who ended up with far worse deals than today. The more you learn, think, and practice negotiating, the better a negotiator you will become. As you achieve better and better results, you will also feel happier, more self-confident, and more in charge of your life.

One of the most powerful ways we learn is to contrast and compare what we are doing with what we *could* be doing. Think of an important area where you are negotiating in your personal or business life today. As you read through this book, think of how you could practice these techniques to achieve a better outcome or result than you are achieving today. As you put these ideas into action, you will be astonished at how much better the negotiation works out for you, and how much happier you will be as a result.

ONE

Everything Is Negotiable

"EVERYTHING IS NEGOTIABLE" should be your attitude and your approach to life and business from now on. One of the greatest obstacles to success and happiness is passivity. Passive people merely accept the current state of affairs, and they usually feel helpless to change the situation. Proactive people, on the other hand, see opportunities and possibilities everywhere, and are always looking for ways to change the situation to their own advantage. This should be your strategy as well.

Think Like a Negotiator

There are very few fixed prices or terms on anything, even if they are written down or printed. You must remember that no matter how firm or inflexible the prices and terms seem to be, everything is negotiable. Your job is simply to find out where and how you can get a better deal than the one that you are being offered.

When people began trading and bartering 6,000 years ago, in ancient Sumeria, it was generally understood that every price was negotiable. In the markets and bazaars of third-world countries, and even in the flea markets and garage sales that may be popular in the neighborhood where you live, every price—either buying or selling—is merely a starting point where the good negotiator begins on the way to getting the very best price possible.

But elsewhere in the modern world, negotiating is not encouraged. It is considered by many people, especially those selling a product or service in the commercial marketplace, to be avoided at all costs. Instead, people print a price list or put a price tag on a product or service and then present this price to you as though it were carved in stone. But a written price doesn't really mean anything. It is not a fixed fact. It is the best-guess *estimate* of someone, somewhere, of how much a person is likely to pay. Any price set by someone can be changed by that person, or by someone else.

Prices Are Arbitrary

The fact is that all pricing is arbitrary. Businesses set their prices based loosely on costs, anticipated profitability, and competitive conditions. As a result, with changing information, all prices can be revised and adjusted in some way. Whenever you see or read about a sale of any kind promoting lower prices, you see an example of the company having guessed wrong when it set the price in the first place.

You should develop the attitude that no matter what the asking price is at the moment, you can improve this deal in some way in your favor. You may be able to get what you want cheaper, faster, or with better terms. Make it a habit to continually look for opportunities to improve the prices or terms in some way.

Contracts Are Merely Starting Points

For example, when you are presented with a contract or an agreement, you are perfectly entitled to cross out or revise any phrases or clauses you don't like. Be aware that any contract presented to you by a vendor (or by anyone else) has been written for and on behalf of the *vendor*. There is very little in the contract that exists to serve your interests in any way. Never allow yourself to be intimidated by the fact that a contract or sales agreement is written down and official looking.

Some years ago, we took out a five-year lease on new space in a new office building. A few years later, the building owner sold the office building to another property company. The new property managers visited each of the tenants and explained that for legal reasons, the tenants would all have to sign a new lease agreement with the new owner. But, we were told, there was nothing to be concerned about. The terms would be more or less the same as the original lease that we had signed, with only a couple of minor alterations.

When we received the new lease for signing, it was about ten pages longer than the original lease. A friend of mine, a commercial office leasing specialist, reviewed it and found fifty-two additions and subtractions from the original lease! And every one of them, without exception, was immediately detrimental or potentially detrimental to our business.

What we did was simple. We went through the new lease agreement and crossed out, revised, and initialed all fifty-two changes. We then returned the marked-up lease to the building owners. A few days later, they came back to us with a clean new contract with all fifty-two revisions made, as we had requested.

The moral of this story: Never allow yourself to be intimidated by the terms or conditions of any sale or purchase agreement. No matter what the other person says or asserts, or writes down in the form of a contract, it is all negotiable. An agreement is merely the first step in the process.

TWO

Overcome Your Negotiation Fears

THE KEY TO getting a better deal is simple. Ask. Ask for a lower price or for better terms and conditions. Ask for revisions and changes in the agreement. Ask for additional inclusions, discounts, concessions, or extra products or services to be included as a part of the overall deal. Ask pleasantly. Ask expectantly. Ask confidently. Ask courteously. Ask adamantly, if you believe it will be more helpful. But always ask definitely and clearly for what you want. Always ask why, and why not? The future belongs to the askers. The future belongs to those people who confidently and boldly ask for what they want, and ask again, and continue to ask.

If this advice is so simple, why is it that so few people step up and ask for what they want? For many of us, it goes back to early childhood. It stems invariably from the *fear of rejection* as the result of criticism and the lack of unconditional love many people experienced as a child. When children do not experience a fully nurturing environment during their formative years, they grow up lacking in self-esteem and self-confidence. As a result, they often don't feel that they deserve to get a better deal than the one they are offered.

This fear of rejection can hold people back throughout their adult lives. They will often accept agreements, conditions of employment, prices—both buying and selling—that are far less advantageous than they could actually accomplish, just because they are afraid that someone will say *no*.

You can overcome a fear by engaging in the *opposite* behavior. If you have a fear of rejection and your normal behavior is to passively accept the terms and conditions offered you, you can overcome this fear by continually asking for a better deal, and by not caring if the person says "no."

Do it repeatedly, and the fear soon diminishes and disappears. This is the process of "systematic desensitization." By confronting your fear, and by repeatedly doing the thing you fear, the fear eventually disappears.

Just as fear is a habit, courage is a habit as well. By forcing yourself to act courageously, especially in asking for better prices and terms in a negotiation, you actually build your own self-confidence and self-esteem.

Cold-Calling Builds Courage

One of the most important lessons in my life came when I began door-to-door selling and cold-calling, hour after hour. At first, I received more rejection than I ever thought possible. Virtually every door I knocked on was closed to me, since I ended up being rejected and told that the person did not want, and was not interested in, my product. I heard the word *no* hundreds, even thousands, of times. Then one day, I asked an experienced salesperson how he dealt with this nonstop rejection. He shared with me these magic words: "Rejection is not personal."

Don't take rejection personally. When someone says "no" to your request in a negotiation, it is not a reflection on you or your personal value. It is not a statement about whether you are a good or a bad person. As far as the person saying no is concerned, it is merely a commercial response to an offer of some kind. It has nothing to do with you. Don't take it *personally*.

Once I learned this key idea, I became a selling machine. I would confidently go from door to door, asking people to buy my product. No matter how many times I heard the word *no*, I just laughed. I realized that the other person was not thinking about me at all. The other person was merely engaging in a knee-jerk reaction that takes place whenever anyone proposes anything that is different from the status quo. Rejection is not personal.

Building an Empire

One of my seminar attendees was a construction worker in Phoenix who decided he wanted to buy older homes and rent them out for enough to pay the mortgage, plus make a profit. But he didn't have very much money to start.

Nonetheless, he began going through the newspaper looking for homes that were put on the market "by owner" instead of being listed with a real estate agent. He began calling on these homeowners and would arrange to view the house, and after determining that it would be a good house to buy, fix up, and rent, he would turn to the owner and offer him 50 percent of the asking price. Some homeowners were angry. Others were furious. But out of every twenty homeowners he called on, one of them was invariably going through a life situation that made the owner a highly motivated seller. There were people whose business had shut down, or who had lost their job, or they were going through a divorce or a bankruptcy, or they had decided to move to another part of the country, and the only thing holding them back was selling their house.

So for every nineteen rejections, someone would counteroffer with a price that was 60 percent or 70 percent of the asking price, which he would eventually accept.

After a few years of his willingness to hear the word *no* over and over again, he owned forty-two houses and was earning more than $10,000 a month. He was on his way to becoming a millionaire. And all because he was not afraid to hear the word *no* when he asked for what he wanted.

Negotiating as a Game

Think of negotiating as a game. It is not a serious, do-or-die matter. It is merely a form of sport. In fact, it is one of the great games in life. Your job is to play the game as skillfully as you possibly can, and then to get better and better at it.

Top negotiators insist upon negotiating on almost every occasion. They haggle and bargain because, for them, it is a form of fun. When you begin to look upon negotiating as an enjoyable activity, and remain calm, confident, and cheerful, you will begin to see opportunities to negotiate on your behalf everywhere you go and in almost everything you do.

THREE

The Types of Negotiating

THERE ARE TWO types of negotiating. Each of them has a different purpose and a different desired outcome. The problem is that they often become confused in the mind of the negotiator, leading to worse results than you could achieve if you were absolutely clear what you were doing and what you wanted to accomplish.

The first type of negotiating, or Type I, is what I'll call a "one-off" style. In this situation, you only plan to negotiate or deal with the other party once, and never again. Each party to the negotiation has only one goal: to get the highest or lowest price and the very best terms and conditions for this one purchase or sale.

Take No Prisoners

In Type I negotiating, you are in an adversarial position with the other person. His goal is to pay you the very least, if buying, or to extract from you the highest possible price, if selling. He is not your friend. No matter how much he smiles, or how polite and courteous he is in the negotiation, he is thinking only about himself and his own benefit or reward. At the end of the day, he does not really care if you pay too much or get too little.

In this type of negotiating, you must be calm, crafty, and selfish. You are entitled to use any possible trick or maneuver to get the best possible deal. Once this transaction is complete, you should assume that you will never see or hear from this person again. It does not matter whether this person likes you, respects you, or wants to be your friend. All that matters is that you get the best deal possible. In later chapters, you will learn a series of strategies and tactics that you can use to increase your success in this type of negotiation.

Long-Term Negotiating

The second style of negotiating is long-term negotiating, or Type II. This is where you intend to enter into a more complex agreement that must be carried out over an extended period of time. In this case, because of the nature of the product, service, contract, or agreement under discussion, you may be working with the same person or organization for many months or years into the future.

Thirty years ago, when I began producing audio and video learning programs with a manufacturer/distributor in Chicago, I was grateful for the company's willingness to market my programs nationally and internationally, and fortunately, the company offered me a set of terms and conditions that were both fair and standard for the industry. Today, thirty years later, I am still working closely with that company and the key people in that organization, from the president on down.

Over the decades, the market has changed, many people have come and gone, and more products have been introduced into the market, become popular, and eventually disappeared. But throughout, my relationship with the key people in that business has been friendly, cordial, polite, and professional. Because I always treated the relationship as a long-term involvement, it has led to some of the best business opportunities and results of my life.

The Chinese Contract

I began using this strategy years ago and have taught it to thousands of businesses and executives who have gone on to use it as well with great satisfaction and excellent results. Let's start by understanding the difference between a standard Western contractual agreement and a Chinese contract.

In the West, an enormous amount of time is spent negotiating the fine print of a contract. "The party of the first part shall do this . . . and the party of the second part shall do that. . . ." This contract, then, becomes the basis for the entire business relationship. Each party is expected to fulfill commitments as stated, word for word, in the written contract. Any deviation from the written contract can lead to breakdowns in the arrangement, penalties, and even litigation.

In the Chinese culture, where I spend a good deal of time each year, the terms and conditions of the agreement are negotiated, discussed, and agreed to. They are then written down on paper, reviewed, revised, and duly signed by both parties.

In a Western contract, this step is the *end* of the discussions or negotiations. But in the Chinese contract, this is the *beginning* of the negotiations and discussions.

In the Chinese mentality, everything that can be thought of or anticipated is written down. But there is a clear understanding that, as the arrangement goes forward, new information will emerge and new situations will arise. This new information and these new situations will necessitate revising the contract so that it is still fair and equitable for both parties.

Whenever I negotiate with a counterpart (and I have agreements with clients in more than sixty countries), we often conclude complex, multipart agreements, involving many thousands of dollars, with a couple of pages.

Right at the beginning, I'll state, "Let us create a *Chinese contract* between us. In this type of contract, you and I will agree on the basic terms and conditions of the business that we will do together. But I want us both to be happy. If at any time something happens that changes the situation around this contract, let us sit down together and renegoti-ate the terms and conditions so that both of us continue to be happy."

And the good news is this: My partners and I have never had an argument, a disagreement, or litigation over one of these "Chinese contracts." In every case, we have remained open, friendly, and focused on maximizing the benefit to each party in the process of our working together.

FOUR

Lifetime Business Relationships

IT IS THE SAME in almost any business. You begin working with a company or an individual, usually at a lower level, and over time, that business relationship can grow into one of the most important parts of your financial and personal life.

Gerard Nierenberg, a past master at professional negotiating, once said the purpose of negotiation is "to reach an agreement such that all parties have their needs satisfied to the degree that they are internally motivated to fulfill their commitments and to enter into subsequent negotiations and transactions with the same party."

Let us break down this definition into its constituent parts. First, "to reach an agreement . . ." means that the purpose of an ongoing negotiation is not to win or lose, not to defeat the opponent, but to reach an agreement of some kind. When both parties begin the negotiating process with a sincere desire to find a way to reach agreement, the behaviors of the two parties are quite different from the onetime negotiating style, and the results are usually far better.

The second part of the definition, ". . . such that all parties have their needs satisfied . . .," recognizes that each party to a negotiation has wants and needs that are different from the other party's. That is why the negotiation or discussion is happening in the first place. For a long-term arrangement, it is essential that both parties look for ways to make sure that the other party's essential needs are satisfied.

Both Parties Must Be Happy

The third part of the definition, ". . . to the degree that they are internally motivated to fulfill their commitments . . .," means that both parties are so happy with the results of the negotiation that they want the ensuing business arrangement to be successful and are more than willing to fulfill the promises they made in the negotiation so that they can enjoy the benefits of the agreement.

Once I was having a conversation with a senior executive of a large learning organization. He told me, quite proudly, that he had negotiated an extremely good deal for his company with a publishing company. He had "ground them down" so much that they finally agreed to advances and royalty terms that were well in excess of what that company was paying its other authors and program developers.

I just happened to be one of this publisher's product developers, and I was surprised to learn that this gentleman had gotten a far better deal in negotiating than I had ever received in working with this same publisher over the years. When I called the president of the company, he explained to me that the other party was quite aggressive and demanding during the negotiation. There was no flexibility or willingness to compromise. Either the publisher agreed to pay the higher rates or this party would not only walk away, but bad-mouth the publisher to others.

The president said, "We did not want any unfriendly people out there in the marketplace, so we politely agreed to their terms and conditions. We now have the exclusive rights to produce and distribute their product, but not the obligation. We have no intention of doing so. Their product will remain on our shelves indefinitely until they come and ask for it back. At that point, we will give it to them and then end our relationship with them permanently."

This senior executive had extracted what appeared to be an excellent, above-market price for his product. But because he lost sight of the importance of the long-term relationship, he and his company ended up with nothing but a contract with a set of prices and terms that the other company had no commitment or motivation to fulfilling.

The Law of Indirect Effort

In negotiating, there is a principle called the Law of Indirect Effort. It says that you achieve more when you act indirectly rather than directly. For example, the harder you try to achieve your own goals in a negotiation, the less successful you will be. When you are clearly striving to achieve the things you want, other people feel compelled to push back to protect and defend themselves.

But the harder you seem to be working to find a way to satisfy the other party (the indirect approach), the more open the other person will be to working to achieve an agreement that is satisfactory to you.

Ralph Waldo Emerson said, "To have a friend, you must first be a friend." By using the Law of Indirect Effort, when you focus on reaching an accord that is in the best interests of the people you are negotiating with, they will relax and start to look for ways to enter into a deal that is satisfactory to you as well.

This is why I always say, "Whatever we decide here today, I want you to be happy. I am open to any ideas and suggestions you have that will ensure you are happy at the end of our discussions, and happy later on as well. Of course, I want to be happy also, but I find that if I focus on your being happy, it will usually work out satisfactorily for me."

This approach almost invariably disarms my negotiating counterpart, and almost invariably we reach an agreement that is satisfactory to both parties. We both walk away happy.

Think About the Future

The fourth and final part of Nierenberg's definition is ". . . and to enter into subsequent negotiations and transactions with the same party." This is the most important part of all in a long-term business arrangement. It means that both parties are so happy with the way that the deal turned out that they are both willing and eager to enter into subsequent agreements over and over again.

Today, the best businesses position themselves as "partners" with their customers, vendors, and suppliers. Instead of spreading their business over a large number of other companies, they consolidate their business with a single supplier with whom they work closely to develop high-quality relationships that lead to better quality, greater efficiency, and eventually, lower prices and higher profits for both parties. This is the strategy used by almost all business leaders in all industries today.

Type II negotiating is a process that has no real beginning, middle, or end, because it goes on continuously. The starting point of this type of negotiation is building quality relationships that are based on trust and credibility. The best business relationships you will ever enter into, whether for sales, purchases, employment, financing, or anything else, will be those based on a contract with which everyone is happy, and that continues in different forms indefinitely.

The worst type of negotiation is one where, when it ends, neither party is satisfied. Neither party wants to negotiate again with the other party. And both parties feel uncomfortable and unmotivated about fulfilling their commitments under the agreement.

FIVE

The Six Styles of Negotiating

THERE ARE SEVERAL different ways to negotiate, but you must be clear about the negotiation style you are using and the output or result that you are striving for.

Win-Lose Negotiating

The first style, called "win-lose negotiating," is when party A gets what he wants and party B loses. This is the aim in Type I negotiating, as discussed in Chapter Three. It is the negotiating approach that is used in a single transaction, where you want to sell at the highest price or buy at the lowest price. Your focus in this type of negotiating is not making friends or establishing long-term relationships. It is simply to get the best deal possible. You do not particularly care if the other person is unhappy or dissatisfied with the price or terms. Your goal is simply to win.

Of course, this is not the kind of negotiating that leads to additional business or transactions, except in special cases, such as when you are pawning your property to get fast cash. In this case, the pawn broker is the winner, paying a fraction of the value of the item, and the person pawning the item is the loser, receiving a fraction.

Lose-Win Negotiating

The second style of negotiating is "lose-win negotiating," and it is the opposite of win-lose negotiating or simply the reverse of the first style. Party B gets what he wants and party A loses. B's needs are satisfied and A's needs are not satisfied. This approach to negotiating is used when each party sees the other party as an opponent or adversary, to be bested with any means available.

Lose-Lose Negotiating

The third approach is "lose-lose negotiating." In this situation, two parties enter into a deal where *neither* one of them is satisfied, because neither party gets much of what was hoped for. This type of negotiating is often accompanied by antagonism, animosity, and arguing.

For example, the husband comes home and says to his wife, "Let's go out for dinner tonight. Where would you like to go?"

She answers that she would like to go out for seafood. He replies that he is sick of seafood and would prefer Italian food. She says that she has had too much Italian food lately and is not interested. To keep peace, they finally agree to go out for Chinese food, which neither of them particularly wants, but it seems like the only compromise that would work in this case.

This is lose-lose negotiating. The wife doesn't get what she wants and neither does the husband. But they accept the results of the negotiation because at least they get something rather than nothing.

Compromise Negotiating

The fourth type of negotiating is called "compromise." In a compromise negotiation, both parties get something and are therefore better off, but neither party's needs are completely met. At the end of the negotiation, both parties walk away with a bad taste in their mouth. They are not so unhappy as to refuse to enter into an agreement, but they are not particularly excited about the results of the negotiation.

No-Deal Negotiating

The fifth style is called "no-deal negotiation." In this situation, you and your counterparty both present your positions, needs, and interests and find that you cannot come to an agreement. You are too far apart. You agree to disagree. You go your separate ways with no animosity or unhappiness. The door remains open for the two of you to negotiate at a later time when conditions are different.

For example, you want to buy a particular item, but the asking price is too high. You offer a lower price but the other party refuses your offer. You are not willing to go any lower, and he is not willing to go any higher. There is no deal.

Win-Win Negotiating

Finally, there is the best kind of deal: a "win-win negotiation." This is what you are aiming for. In a win-win negotiation, both parties feel that they have won. Both parties feel that they have entered into an excellent deal. Both parties are happy, satisfied, and eager to fulfill their commitments and to enter into additional deals on the same or similar bases.

In most cases, win-win negotiating requires coming to a third alternative that is better than either had initially thought of. Both parties enter into the negotiation with a series of ideas, interests, and positions fixed in their minds. Often they find that it is impossible to compromise between the two separate positions. But then they find a third alternative that is in most cases different from what either party had thought about when they entered into the negotiation in the first place.

A win-win negotiation occurs when the third alternative turns out to be superior to what either party had come to the table with in the first place.

Look for a Win-Win Solution

Some time ago, I was negotiating a real estate development agreement for 330 homes with the members of the town council. My clients had purchased the property on the edge of the town and had done all the design work for the subdivision. However, the town fathers were demanding $10,000 per lot, a total of $3.3 million in cash, upfront, for offsite improvements. This was not an unreasonable amount because the town would have to spend a lot of money to accommodate the new subdivision. The problem was that my clients did not have the cash to pay upfront.

Just when it appeared that we had reached an impasse, and my clients were beginning to think the deal was slipping through their fingers, I proposed a win-win solution. "It seems the final point has to do with the $3.3 million," I said. "Here is my solution. We hereby agree to give you the $3.3 million that you request."

Then, I went on to say, "We will agree to everything we have discussed over the last three days, including paying the town $3.3 million, but we need one small concession from you. We would ask that you agree to receive the $3.3 million at the rate of $10,000 per lot as we sell them to home builders and developers."

There was silence in the room. Finally, the mayor broke the silence. "Well, of course we would like to get the entire amount upfront," he said, "but if partial payment as you sell the lots is the best you can do, we can live with that."

The deal was done.

The reason I tell this story is because this is the sort of thing that happens over and over again when you seek a win-win solution. Be prepared to think outside of the box. Be clear about what each party absolutely must have in a negotiation, and then see if you can't find a way to achieve those mutual goals so that everyone feels like a winner.

SIX

The Uses of Power in Negotiating

YOU ALMOST ALWAYS have more power in a negotiation than you think you have. Even when you feel that the other person has all the power, it may be that you have something that he wants, or you can find something that he wants that will swing the balance of power back in your favor.

There are several ways that you can increase your power in a negotiation, including through preparation, authority, knowledge of the other party, empathy, rewarding/punishing, and investment.

The Power of Preparation

The more thoroughly prepared and knowledgeable you are when you go into a negotiation, the greater power you will have. Do your homework. Robert Ringer, a skilled negotiator, talks about taking an accountant, lawyer, and a business manager to a negotiation with a single real estate owner. This created the perception of overwhelming competence and knowledge of the transaction under discussion.

The Power of Authority

Making it clear that you have the authority to buy or not buy—to make or not make a buying decision—gives you power. Also, when you make it clear that you are knowledgeable in this field, and that you are quite clear and experienced about exactly what the price, terms, and conditions should be, it often intimidates the other person into giving you a better deal.

The Power of Knowledge of the Needs of the Other Party

The more you know about the situation of the other party, the greater strength you have in a negotiation. If you discover that the other person has a pressing need for a product or service that you can offer, or that the other company has serious financial problems and needs capital or credit, you are in a stronger position to negotiate an excellent deal.

The Power of Empathy or Identification

This a power used by top negotiators in almost every area. The more time you take to establish a warm relationship with the other person, the more likely your opponent will be relaxed and open to negotiating with you on better terms.

The Power of Rewarding and Punishing

This is an essential power that you can and should develop in a negotiation. When you have the ability to confer rewards or benefits on someone, or to withhold rewards and benefits, they are far more likely to do business with you. They will want to negotiate with you.

The Power of Investment

This refers to the amount of time and effort that you or the other person has spent in this negotiation. If you have only spent five minutes, then there is little investment on your part. But if you have spent five days, weeks, or months over time working toward an agreement, you have made a substantial investment, and it makes a definite impression on the other party. The greater the investment of the other party, or yourself, the greater power you have in the negotiation.

SEVEN

Power and Perception

POWER IS ALL about perception. It is not the power you have but the power the other person thinks you have that counts.

A good friend of mine, once worth many millions of dollars, lost all his money in the Great Recession. He was forced to cut back in every area, including selling his large yacht and his home in the exclusive Hamptons.

But he never told anyone.

Today, he is on his way back. He is buying and selling, negotiating and trading, expanding one company and selling another. Because everyone believes that he is still wealthy, he carries himself as though he has the same financial clout that he had a few years ago. Perception is everything.

The importance of perception applies to the types of power used in negotiating, as described in the previous chapter. Here are some other ways that *perceived power* can influence negotiations.

The Power of Scarcity
Often people don't know how much they want to acquire a product or service until it appears that they won't be able to get it at all. The perception that you have something scarce that other people need, and that other people want and are prepared to buy immediately, gives you excellent bargaining power in a negotiation.

The Power of Indifference
You cultivate an attitude of indifference by remaining calm and unemotional during the negotiation, thereby creating the perception that you don't really care whether you buy or sell the product. This is often called a "poker face."

When you watch the poker champions on TV, you will notice that their faces remain calm and they appear almost bored throughout the game. It is even better if the other party is eager to make the deal, one way or another. If you are indifferent and the other person is not, you are going to get a better deal.

The Power of Courage
You demonstrate courage in your willingness to take a strong position on a deal, to make a clear and unequivocal offer or

demand, to risk the failure of the negotiation, and to walk away from a deal if necessary. When the other party sees that you are completely confident in what you are doing and what you are offering, it often intimidates them into giving you a better price or terms.

The Power of Commitment

If the other party sees that you are totally committed to concluding the transaction and making the deal, and that you will do whatever is necessary to achieve it, you develop the perception of power.

During World War II, the British Army had 80,000 troops in Singapore and was well supplied to fight off an invasion. Yet, with fewer forces, the Japanese took Singapore from the British. They convinced the British that they were so committed to victory that they would overrun the island and kill everyone on it, including civilians. Because the Japanese had already overrun all of Malaysia, causing large casualties, the British had no reason to doubt their commitment to overrun Singapore. This perception of Japan's determination caused the British to capitulate.

The Power of Knowledge and Expertise

The party with the greatest perceived knowledge or expertise has tremendous power in a negotiation. If you are selling a complex or sophisticated product or service, your command of background data or technology gives you a distinct advantage over a buyer with a lower level of knowledge about the product or service.

The most successful retail businesses in the world are the Apple stores. While Tiffany & Co. of New York has an average sale of about $2,000 per square foot, the average sale in an Apple store is $4,600 per square foot. Why? Because the people who work at Apple stores are so incredibly knowledgeable about the products and services they sell that people pay hundreds and thousands of dollars to buy products that they never even knew they wanted when they walked in the door.

The Impact of Emotions on Negotiation

EMOTION IS A KEY factor in negotiations. Emotions, especially the emotions of *desire*, *greed*, *fear*, or *anger*, can help or hurt you in a negotiation. The more you can keep your emotions out of the negotiating process, the more capable you will be of getting the best deal for yourself or your organization. The more emotional you become, the less capable you will be of negotiating well on your own behalf.

Emotions distort valuations. You are incapable of thinking clearly and making good decisions when you let your emotions take over. Everything you do to stay calm during a negotiation will help you to get a better deal.

How Badly Do You Want It?

The most powerful emotion in negotiating is *desire*. The more you want to purchase or acquire a particular product or service, or to sell something, the less power you will have in negotiating.

If you want something so badly that you can taste it, you are likely to pay almost any price. If the other person knows how badly you want something, he will have an advantage over you.

Remember the power of *indifference* mentioned in the previous chapter? Ask yourself some questions. What would happen if you didn't acquire this product at all? What is the worst thing that could happen if you were unable to succeed in this negotiation or purchase? If you didn't get it, would it kill you?

Prepare yourself in advance for not achieving the object of your desire at all. The calmer you are about the idea of not succeeding in the negotiation, whether buying or selling, the better you will be able to think, and the better decisions you will make.

Control Your Emotions

Greed is another emotion that exerts an inordinate effect on your thinking. The idea of getting something for nothing, or acquiring something at a cost or price substantially less than you thought you were going to pay, can distort your emotions and make it difficult for you to think clearly. The very idea of getting something that you don't deserve, or something that seems like a terrific deal, can hurt your ability to make a rational decision.

Next to desire and greed, *fear* is the most dangerous of emotions. The more fearful you are about an outcome, the more easily you will be excited into taking an action that may not be in your best interests. This is why indifference to whether or not you acquire a certain object, or achieve a certain result in a negotiation, is a wonderful way of calming your emotions.

Finally, another major emotion that can cause you to make poor decisions in negotiating is *anger*. Fear and anger are often used by manipulative negotiators to get people worked up and to stampede them into making a decision that is not good for them.

Keep Calm at All Times

Whenever you feel yourself becoming emotional in any negotiation, call for a "time-out." Take a break. Go for a walk. Come back after lunch or on another day. Discipline yourself not to make an important decision or to agree to a condition when you are in the grip of an emotion of any kind.

Ask yourself the question, "So what?" If the deal collapses or doesn't work out, so what? A mentor of mine, a very successful businessman, once told me something I never forgot. When I would become excited about a potential business deal, he would say, "Brian, deals are like buses. There will always be another one coming along. Don't get excited or worried about this one. If it doesn't come together smoothly, forget about it. Something else will come along."

A wise man once told me, "Sometimes the very best deals are the ones that you don't get into at all."

Practice Detachment

The key to governing your emotions is to prepare yourself psychologically, in advance. Practice detachment. When you go into a negotiation, breathe deeply. Watch yourself carefully and remain calm, like a Buddhist. Don't get emotionally involved or identify too strongly with the deal.

Your ability to maintain a sense of calm, clear detachment is the key to maintaining a position of strength. Remember that the person who is the most emotionally involved in the achievement of a particular outcome is the one who has the least power.

NINE

The Element of Time in Decisions

TIME AND TIMING are key factors in effective negotiating. Very often, you can get an excellent deal in a negotiation if you plan the timing carefully in advance.

The Secret Is Out

For example, when purchasing a new car, there is a strategy you can use. Salespeople and sales managers have quotas to fulfill each month. If you visit a dealership in the first three weeks of a month, they are not yet under any pressure to fulfill their quota. Because of this, they will ask for the highest possible prices and will be the least flexible in negotiating.

The best time to buy a car is in the last two or three days of the month. You can go to the dealership earlier to test-drive and select the car that you want to purchase. But wait

until the last two or three days of the month to begin negotiating the final price, terms, and conditions. You will always
get a better deal, and sometimes a vastly better deal.

Some years ago I was giving a sales seminar to more than
1,000 people. I mentioned this factor of timing with regard
to buying a car as a casual comment to the people in the
audience who might be thinking of buying a car in the
future. To my amazement, there turned out to be almost 100
car salesmen from different companies spread throughout
the audience. They were furious at my "revelation." When
the seminar was over, they chased me down the street shout-
ing and swearing at me for having given away one of the best
kept secrets in automobile sales.

Beware a Sense of Urgency

Perhaps the most important factor in timing has to do with
a sense of urgency. The more urgently you want to purchase
something, the less bargaining power you have. Good salespeople and negotiators use every device to create a sense of
urgency to weaken their customers' ability to negotiate
effectively on their behalf.

"If we cannot come to an agreement today," the salesperson says, "the entire price changes tomorrow morning." Or,
"We have a special on this particular item, but it ends today
at five o'clock. After that, it goes back to full price."

To counter this technique, when someone says that you
must make a decision immediately or you will lose special
terms or conditions, you reply by saying: "If I have to make a

decision immediately, the answer is *no*. But if I have an opportunity to consider your offer carefully, the answer may be different."

Earlier in American history, fire departments were privately owned and staffed by local shopkeepers. When a person's home was on fire, the homeowner would send someone to the fire department to request a fire truck as soon as possible. When the fire truck arrived at the burning home, the owner of the fire truck would then negotiate with the homeowner the charging price to put out the fire. As you can imagine, the homeowner was not in a position to bargain very well on his own behalf. It was because of this imbalance that all fire departments eventually became city owned and managed.

Don't Rush into a Decision

Another manipulative technique is "rushing." It occurs when the other party tries to rush you or hurry you into making a decision before you have a chance to give it much thought. Whenever someone tries to rush you into a decision, you can counter by saying, "I need more time to think about this decision. I will let you know at a later date."

Excellent negotiators, in fact, use time to delay. Delay is the cruelest form of denial. The more you delay a negotiation or a resolution for a person who wants to come to some kind of conclusion, the greater strength you have.

Delay in reaching an agreement is a powerful technique that you can use to protect yourself. Put off serious decisions for at least twenty-four hours to allow for reflection and further consideration. The more you delay the making of a decision in a negotiation, the better your ability to make a better decision. The final deal that you get will improve as well.

Set and Avoid Deadlines

Another helpful device with regard to time and timing is deadlines. Wherever possible, give the other party a set deadline for decision making. Tell the other party that if you do not have a decision by a specific time or date, all bets are off. The price, terms, and conditions will change. You will sell the product or service to someone else.

Herb Cohen, a master negotiator and teacher of negotiating, tells a story about a valuable lesson he learned early in his career as an executive.

He was sent to Japan to negotiate a large manufacturing contract. This potential business arrangement was important to his company and to himself as a young executive.

When he arrived in Japan, his hosts picked him up in a limousine, drove him to his hotel, and told him that they would take care of everything during his visit as their honored guest. They asked him for his plane tickets so that they would know when he was departing and they could arrange for travel back to the airport. As a result, they knew that he had six days in Japan before he had to leave and return to the United States.

For the first five days, they lavishly wined and dined him. They took him to the plant and toured him around. But they never discussed business. Because of their courtesy, he attempted to be as polite as possible in return. But they didn't get down to serious negotiating until the final day. They were still negotiating the final details in the car on the way to the airport. He accepted a far worse deal than he ever would have gotten if he had realized that they were using time against him.

The 20/80 Rule in Negotiating

In negotiation and in timing, the 80/20 rule applies in a special sense. This rule says that the last 20 percent of any negotiation will deal with 80 percent of the important issues and the value of the entire transaction. The first 80 percent of a negotiation will only deal with 20 percent of the issues to be decided.

You must accept that the first 80 percent of the discussion will revolve around unimportant issues. It is only near the end of the negotiation, when time is running out, that you will get down to, discuss, and finally agree upon the most important issues under consideration.

What I have learned is that you must be patient during the first part of the negotiation. There is no point in trying to rush. If you have two hours to discuss a transaction, the most important points will be decided in the last thirty minutes. Be patient.

TEN

Know What You Want

IT IS AMAZING how many people enter into a negotiation without knowing precisely what they want to achieve, and so they make up their goals and desires as they go along. They are easily influenced, persuaded, and manipulated to buy or sell at higher or lower prices.

The solution for this predicament is for you to think through your ideal desired outcomes in advance. Ask yourself the question, "If this negotiation worked out perfectly for me, what result would I achieve?"

Think on paper. Write out and describe everything that you want, in advance. People who know exactly what they want, and have written it down, have a distinct advantage over those who are vague or unsure.

Discuss It with Others

Whenever possible, discuss the upcoming negotiation with someone else and explain the details of a perfect outcome. This exercise of discussing with others and thinking on paper doesn't mean that you will get the product or service for free, or that you will achieve a goal that disadvantages another person. However, by thinking through the negotiation in advance, you are much more likely to reach a win-win outcome with which you and the other person will be satisfied.

As part of this process, determine the price that you are going to have to pay to achieve the ideal outcome. What are you prepared to give or concede in order to get what you want in this negotiation or transaction?

Best, Medium, and Worst Outcomes

Think in terms of three levels of possible outcomes: best, medium, and worst. When you go into a bargaining session, you should have these three outcomes in mind and aim for the best possible price and terms from the beginning.

You will often be amazed at what happens when you start with the highest possible price for selling and the lowest possible price for buying. Sometimes, due to factors over which you have no control, the other party will agree with you immediately, and no further bargaining is necessary.

The medium outcome you have defined is acceptable, and the third possible outcome is the worst that could happen. If you are driven back to accept the worst, this is the lowest you would go and still proceed with the transaction. This is called your "ultimate fallback position." You will fall back to this level even though you would hate to do it, but it is the lowest you will go before walking away. Below this level, you would not proceed. So determine clearly, in advance, the least you will accept so that you are fully prepared.

Start at the Top (or Bottom)

Where do you start bargaining in a negotiation? You start slightly above your very best or optimal result. You may have to make concessions along the way and end up at a lower level, but always start off at the very best level that you would wish to achieve.

Labor negotiators are famous for using this tactic. In union contract negotiations, the negotiators start off with a demand for a 50 percent increase in pay in one year, plus improvements to medical care, pensions, and other benefits. They present this offer as their minimum demand for a new union contract.

By the time the dust has settled, they have accepted a 5 percent pay increase over two years, with no improvements to medical or pension plans. They then go back to their membership and hail this as a great victory.

Think through your best-, medium-, and worst-case positions in advance so that you are absolutely clear about what you want and what you will not accept. Then begin with your ideal outcome and negotiate down (or up) from there.

ELEVEN

The Harvard Negotiation Project

HARVARD FACULTY and staff have studied thousands of large and small negotiations, both in business and in national and international politics. They identified four key elements to successful negotiating. (The entire Harvard Negotiation Project is explained in the book *Getting to Yes: Negotiating Agreement Without Giving In,* by Roger Fisher, William Ury, and Bruce Patton.)

1. *People.* A key to successful negotiating is to separate the personalities of the people from the problem and the issues at hand. Remain unemotional. Keep your mind and your eyes focused on the subject of the negotiation, and don't allow yourself to be sidetracked by the personalities, either positive or negative.

2. *Interests.* Begin the negotiation by clearly identifying the interests or needs of the different parties to the negotiation. Before you write out a list of what you want, write a list of the outcomes you are trying to accomplish. Then you decide what you will have to get in the negotiation in order to accomplish your goals.

   When you sit down with the different parties, and even before, take the time to develop absolute clarity about what the other party wants and needs to achieve from this negotiation. Ask them, "If this discussion was ideal, what result would we achieve at the end, in your estimation?"

3. *Options.* Before getting into an argument on various points, develop a variety of options in those areas where you disagree. Create several possibilities. Use brainstorming methods to develop alternative approaches. You can use a mind map, a whiteboard, or a flipchart.

4. *Criteria.* These are often called "boundary conditions." Before you negotiate, agree to base the result or conclusion on some objective criteria. How are you going to decide whether you have come up with a good ideal for both parties? What are you trying to avoid, achieve, or preserve?

Once you are both clear on what you need to accomplish in the negotiation to make both parties happy, you then compare various options and conclusions against this desired end result. You say, "A good deal will satisfy *this* condition. It will give us *that* result. It will achieve *this* goal." In other words, you state what a good deal will look like, both for you and for the other party.

Finally, you go through and discuss the various ways that you can achieve the interests and the needs that will fulfill the objective criteria or boundary conditions that you have established.

This is a powerful process of negotiating that keeps people's minds focused solely on the objectives and prevents them from being steered off course by personalities and tangential issues.

TWELVE

Preparation Is the Key

PREPARATION IS THE true mark of the professional. Eighty percent of all negotiating success, if not more, is based on thorough preparation on your part before the first conversation takes place.

Begin by considering the subject matter: What are you going to talk about? What is the purpose of this negotiation? Define clearly what you want to achieve and what issues are on the table.

What are your objectives or goals for this negotiation? What do you want to accomplish when you go into this discussion? The greater clarity you have about your goals, the faster you will achieve them, and the easier it is to convey them to the other party.

Options Mean Freedom

Having options may be your best friend in getting the best deal in any negotiation. The more options you have, the freer you are to make the best decision. In a negotiation you are only as free as your well-developed options.

If you have not developed options in advance, your only choice in a negotiation is to agree with what the other party offers. Your hands are tied. But if you have a variety of options, or different ways that you can go, you will then have a great deal of strength, power, and bargaining leverage. Develop as many alternatives as possible well in advance, and on paper. Think them through carefully before the negotiation begins.

Continually Develop More Options

Do your homework and research to find other sources for the product or service under consideration. Find out what you should pay for it, and what the times and dates of delivery could be. With multiple options, you can go into a negotiation calm and relaxed, which allows you to leverage the power of indifference throughout the negotiation. When you have a series of well-developed options, you are completely free to accept or reject the terms and conditions of the other person. You will always get a better deal as a result.

Learn Everything You Can

One of the key parts of preparation is doing some homework on the people you are negotiating with. Today, the best tool for pre-call preparation is the Internet, especially Google. It s amazing how much you can find out with a couple of mouse clicks.

Often, you know someone else who has negotiated or done business with these people. Phone them, explain your situation, and ask for advice. Sometimes, one word of advice or insight can give you an advantage in the upcoming negotiation.

Make a Few Phone Calls

A friend of mine was considering purchasing a manufacturing company. This company had a line of products that would fit perfectly with his company. The owner of the other company was demanding several million dollars for his business, plus stiff terms and conditions after the purchase.

My friend called his banker and asked if he knew anyone at the bank of the other company owner. As usually happens, bankers know other bankers, and he phoned the banker of the person wanting to sell his company. He discovered, privately, that the company was in serious financial difficulty; if management did not find a purchaser or source of new finance within a few days, the company would be shut down by the bank.

With this piece of information, my friend was able to sit down with the demanding and blustery company owner and negotiate an extraordinarily good deal. He was able to buy the company for no money down, taking over the existing indebtedness, and pay out the owner over time with profits generated from the business.

Question Assumptions

Peter Drucker wrote that "errant assumptions lie at the root of every failure."

Incorrect assumptions are one of the main reasons for disagreement and misunderstandings in a negotiation. Much of the time that is spent in a negotiation is taken up resolving incorrect assumptions of some kind.

Before you begin the negotiations, ask, "What are my assumptions?" More specifically: What are your *obvious* assumptions? What are your *hidden* assumptions? What are the obvious and hidden assumptions of the other party? Are your counterparties assuming that you really want to enter into this agreement? Are they assuming that you are indifferent, friendly, or hostile? Are they assuming that you are a good person or a difficult person to deal with?

Test Your Assumptions

Most of all, could your assumptions be wrong? What if they were? If your major assumptions going into this negotiation were wrong, how would you have to change your demands or position?

One of the assumptions we have when entering into a negotiation is that the other party actually wants to conclude a deal. Sometimes, this is not the case. Others may be negotiating with you only to improve their negotiating position with the party they really want to deal with. They simply want to negotiate with you to find out the best deal they can get before they make the deal they desire with someone else.

Therefore, think about how you can clarify each other's assumptions before you get into the details of the negotiation.

Identify the Main Issues

Finally, in preparing for the negotiation, ask, What are the main issues? Where do we differ in wants or needs? What are the areas of conflict or disagreement? What details need to be discussed and resolved?

The more carefully you prepare in advance of a negotiation, the greater strength you will have, and the better the deal that you will get. The key to preparation is to do your homework. Get the facts. Get the real facts, not the assumed facts. Knowledge is power.

THIRTEEN

Clarify Your Positions— and Theirs

YOUR POSITIONS are the starting points. They include where you are coming from, where you are going, and how much or how little you can or will accept. These are your criteria or "boundary conditions," as described in the Harvard Negotiation Project chapter. They are the constraints, the limits, the factors that must be dealt with and resolved in the agreement.

Your position consists of your best and worst outcomes, plus the minimum and maximum range of prices and terms that you can accept in reaching an agreement.

Clarity Is King

What are your essential conditions for a successful negotiation? What must you get out of this process in order to make it worthwhile? What are the most important things that you must not give up, no matter what happens? And what are you willing to concede in order to get your essentials?

What sort of tie-in concessions can you ask for or offer? The rule is to never give a concession in a negotiation without requesting another concession in return. If you concede anything in a negotiation without requesting something in return, the other party will consider this a sign of weakness and will demand additional concessions for that reciprocation.

Know What You Are Dealing With

What are the essential desires or outcomes of the other party? Do everything possible to discover and consider the other side's minimums and maximums. What must they absolutely achieve or receive in this negotiation?

Some time ago, I negotiated a lease for office space. In my pre-negotiation analysis, after some research, I found that the owner could only lease the premises under certain terms and conditions. He had to receive a certain amount in the lease agreement or the mortgage holder would not approve it. With this information, I knew that the owner's essentials were within specific parameters.

There were many factors in the lease agreement that could be negotiated by the landlord. But the basic rent was controlled by the mortgage holder. I could discuss the amount of free rent, parking, and so on with the building owner, but the rent had to be at a specific minimum or no approval was possible.

I also knew that the building owner was going through certain financial difficulties, and in order to keep the building, he had to lease out more than 80 percent of the building within a short time. Knowing the owner's essential requirements made it possible for me to negotiate a much better lease in terms of tenant improvements, common-area expenses, and parking for my staff.

REVERSING THE SITUATION

One of the best ways to improve the results of any negotiation is for you to argue the case of your opponent before you begin preparing your own case.

In law school, students are taught to take the case of the opposing party and put together a complete argument based on the facts of the case as if they were acting for the other party. Only after they have prepared the case for the other party do they prepare their own case.

This exercise enables an aspiring lawyer or negotiator to think through honestly and objectively the strengths and weaknesses of the opponent in a negotiation. This same technique can give you a far better perspective on what you will be discussing with your counterparties, enabling you to anticipate what they are likely to ask for and the strength of their arguments.

Always reverse the situation before you begin. Put yourself in the position of the other party. Imagine that you are the other person and you want to get the best deal possible out of this negotiation. If you were the other person, what would you be asking for? What are the strengths and weaknesses of your position? What is more important, and what is less important?

LESSONS FROM NEGOTIATING A LEASE

When I was negotiating a new office lease, I was up against a landlord who was difficult and demanding.

My weakness was that I wanted the convenience of staying in my existing offices, but I did not want to be tied to a five-year lease. I wanted the flexibility of being able to move to larger space or to downsize if necessary.

Before the negotiation, I sat down with a piece of paper and wrote out everything that I could think of that the landlord would ask for. My list came to about twenty items. Then, I prepared my own side of the negotiation on another sheet of paper.

To this day, I look back in some amazement at how much better a deal I was able to negotiate by thinking through his position in advance. Instead of spending several hours in discussion, we managed to resolve all the issues in about thirty minutes.

Think It Through in Advance

In each negotiation where I have used this technique, the results have been the same. I have always gotten a better deal for myself and created a win-win situation for both of us. Remember that, in a negotiation, each party has issues that are extremely important and other issues that are of medium to low importance. The reason that a negotiation is successful is that both parties are able to achieve their most important goals while compromising on the less important goals. By writing all of these large and small goals on paper before you begin, you will think with greater clarity, negotiate with greater effectiveness, and get a better deal.

Ideal Outcomes for All

Some years ago, I was preparing to fly to New York to negotiate a contract that would result in revenues to me in the hundreds of thousands of dollars. I sat down with a piece of paper and wrote out exactly what the ideal solution would be for me.

We had set aside an entire day to negotiate the terms of this contract. But instead of starting with the contract, I instead asked my counterparts, "If this discussion was completely successful, what would be the perfect outcome for you?"

They were a bit surprised at the question, but they answered honestly. If this contract discussion worked out perfectly well, they said, it would be at this price (which they stated) and these terms. That would be ideal for them and, in their mind, ideal for me.

In return, I told them what would be the ideal outcome for me, which was not very far off from their goal for the negotiation. We quickly agreed on all of the small details and then finalized the major issues. Instead of eight hours, the entire discussion took less than two hours, and everybody was happy and satisfied at the end.

FOURTEEN

The Law of Four

IN REVIEWING thousands of negotiations, both simple and complicated, we find that there are usually only four main issues to be decided in any negotiation. There will be many smaller issues, but there are usually only four *main* ones. Occasionally, there may be one, two, three, or even five main issues, but this law says that there are usually only four. Your job is to think through and identify what those four issues might be, both for yourself and for the other party, and what you can do to deal effectively with them.

There will be a *primary* issue that is most important to the individual, and there will be three *minor* issues, each of which is important, but not as important as the main issue.

When you buy a house, for instance, your first concern will be the house itself—its layout, attractiveness, and condition.

Then, you will be concerned about price, financing and terms, what's included in the purchase, when you can take occupancy, and other details. When you go to buy a new car, as another example, your primary issue is usually the model, color, and size of the car. But since the same car can be purchased from more than one dealership, the subjects to be negotiated will be price, value of trade-in, accessories, and/or terms of payment. Once you have decided on a particular car, your primary issue will probably be the total price of the car. Then, you will negotiate over the trade-in value of your existing car, the accessories, and the interest rate and payment terms.

Stalemate in Negotiating

In a negotiation, each party has a number-one issue that is different from the other party's. If both parties have the same issue as their primary concern, it becomes extremely difficult to negotiate or to reach an agreement.

For example, since 1947 in the Middle East, there have been negotiations going on between the Israelis and the Palestinians. The major issue for both parties is the land of Israel and the existence of the state of Israel. The number-one issue for the Israelis is the continued existence of their state. The number-one issue for the Palestinians is the abolition of the Israeli state. As long as these remain the primary positions of both parties, negotiations can go on for decades, but no resolution is possible.

Your Primary Issue

The Law of Four is a tremendous mental tool in a negotiation. It gives you a greater sense of clarity. By identifying your primary issue, and the other party's primary issue, you can often find a win-win understanding where both parties get the most important thing they want from the negotiation. You can then negotiate and concede on the smaller issues.

There is one final point about the Law of Four. It seems that the major issues for both parties are the ones that will be agreed to last. The 20/80 rule applies in negotiating. The last 20 percent of a negotiation includes 80 percent of the most important issues under discussion.

Agree on the Noncontroversial Issues

Previously, I described a real estate negotiation that involved a lengthy development agreement containing fifty-two changes. What I had found in negotiating this type of agreement is a technique or tactic that is extremely effective: Go through the entire agreement, from the first page to the last page, and discuss every clause, condition, term, and issue where there may be a difference of opinion or desire.

You will find that you and the other party will largely agree on about 80 percent of the terms and conditions in a contract, no matter how large. When you come to a term or a condition where there is disagreement, agree to pass over it for the time being and go on to the next clause or condition where you have no disagreement. When you've gone through the entire agreement, go through the agreement again, from front to back, and revisit the issues where there is disagreement. In the second iteration, you will begin to find ways to concede, compromise, and trade to resolve these issues. But there will still be issues that remain unresolved.

Then, you go through the agreement a third time, and a fourth time if necessary. At a certain point, you will come down to the "final four." You will reach the stage where there are four issues, with one major issue that must be resolved, and three minor issues. Now, you are ready to do some serious negotiating.

Terms of Employment

In applying for a new job, your negotiation for salary and benefits can have a major effect on how much you earn and how happy you are at that job for years to come.

Most people start off thinking that their primary concern is to get the highest salary possible from the beginning. But many companies have constraints on how much they can pay for a particular job. Quite often, an employer will not be able to match your salary expectations. In that case, you shift gears. You negotiate for more benefits, such as a company car, better health plan, more time off than is required by law, flexible working hours, and other details that are important.

One of the best strategies is to agree with the salary offered, once you find out that the employer is inflexible, and then get agreement on what you will have to do or accomplish to get an increase in pay. It is important that you get the employer to agree to do a review within ninety days;

if you have achieved certain benchmarks, which are identified in writing and defined numerically, then you will get an increase of a certain amount. This is a good negotiating strategy when you are taking on a new job of any kind.

FIFTEEN

The Power of Suggestion in Negotiating

HUMAN BEINGS are greatly influenced by their environments, and by the power of suggestion contained in people and situations around them.

Fully 95 percent of your thinking, feeling, and decision making are influenced by or completely controlled by your suggestive environment. Your job is 1) to be aware of the suggestive influences around you and the impact they can have on your thinking, and on the thinking of the other party, and then 2) to do everything possible to control those elements.

Take, for example, *location*. The location in which a negotiation takes place can have a major impact on the terms and conditions agreed upon. When you are in someone else's office and surrounded by the other person's furniture, personnel, and other elements, you automatically suffer a disadvantage in negotiating on your own behalf. You are at a distinct psychological disadvantage because you are outside of your comfort zone, and the other person is firmly planted in her comfort zone. The other person will have greater confidence and a feeling of personal power, and you will have less confidence and a lesser feeling of power.

Change the Location

You will see quite often that in serious negotiations, such as in labor/management relations, politics, and especially complex business deals, the parties will agree to go to a separate location that is neutral and outside the comfort zone of either of them. This puts both parties on an equal footing in terms of the suggestive impact of their environment.

Something as simple as offering to discuss an issue over coffee or lunch at the local diner is superior to negotiating something serious in the other person's office or boardroom or any other setting where that person has a psychological advantage.

The Power of Personality

Personality is another suggestive element. The best type of personality in a negotiation is *empathetic*, *warm*, and *friendly*. The more comfortable you feel with the other person, the more open and responsive you will be to that person's requests in a negotiation. The opposite is also true. The more friendly and pleasant you are, the more likely it is that you will get a better deal than if you were reserved or abrasive.

Empathy has been identified as the number-one psychological quality of top salespeople. People who are the best at helping others enter into business transactions seem to have high degrees of empathy. They are liked and respected by the other person, and the other person feels comfortable entering into arrangements with them.

Positioning and Body Language

Another suggestive element is positioning and body language. According to Albert Mehrabian of UCLA, 55 percent of your communication with another person is contained in your body language—the way you physically move and position yourself relative to the other person.

The basic rule with regard to physical positioning is to avoid sitting across the table from the person you are negotiating with. When you sit directly across a table or a desk, you automatically put yourself in an adversarial position. The unconscious message is that the two of you are enemies and are about to "do battle" of some kind. Over the years, I have found that sitting at a round table with the other person or sitting kitty-corner are far better positions for achieving agreement.

Your Hands Convey a Message

Another negotiating factor, or suggestive influence in negotiating with regard to body language, is the way you hold your hands and arms, and the way you move your body. For example, when you fold your arms, you appear to be closing yourself off to the arguments of the other person. You signal that you are rejecting or disagreeing with what the person is saying.

One of the universal symbols of openness, honesty, and sincerity is open hands. When you sit with your arms unfolded and your hands out, palms up, in a negotiation, you suggest that what you are saying is reasonable, acceptable, friendly, and poses no threat to the other person.

When you lean forward, pay close attention to the other party, focus on the person's mouth when he's speaking, and nod, you create a positive, warm impression of an interested and sincere person who genuinely wants to find an agreement that is acceptable to everyone involved.

Other Suggestive Elements

- *Comfort.* You are more likely to negotiate a better deal if your physical surroundings—the furniture, lighting, temperature—are comfortable.

- *Rest or Fatigue.* You are always more likely to negotiate effectively if you are well rested before you go into the discussion.

- *Food, Hunger, and Thirst.* When you eat well before starting a negotiation, your brain is able to function at its best. Likewise with hydration. The best brain foods are high in protein of some kind. Avoid bread, bagels, bacon, sausage, or cooked meats, all of which will actually make you feel drowsy halfway through the morning. Negotiating after sharing a meal with the other party is also a powerful suggestive technique. Whenever we share a meal with another person, we almost always feel better about the other person and warmer toward that person. We like people more when we share something with them.

- *Your Attitude.* The final element in the power of suggestion in negotiating is your attitude. In a negotiation, a positive attitude—defined as a general cheerfulness and sense of optimism—is much more effective than a negative attitude in getting you the results that you want.

SIXTEEN

Persuasion by Reciprocation

IN HIS BOOK, *Influence*, Robert Cialdini lists the factors that have the greatest impact on the way people think and respond to you. The most powerful of all influences, in his estimation, is the power of *reciprocity*. Extensive research shows that reciprocity—giving and receiving—is the most powerful way to gain agreement and commitment.

Human beings tend to be *fair* in their interactions with others. This means that when you do something for me, I feel obligated to reciprocate, to do something for you of equal or greater value. This is a natural and normal human instinct. It is the basis of civilization, and the foundation of the Law of Contract, which makes all business possible.

Do Things for Others

What this means in a negotiation is that whenever you do something nice for other people, even holding their chair or personally getting them a cup of coffee, you trigger within them an unconscious desire to reciprocate—to pay you back in a positive way for your kindness.

Whenever you ask other people about their life, work, or family, and listen with genuine interest while they talk, it makes them feel happy about themselves.

Use the Socratic Method

To trigger reciprocity, use the Socratic method of negotiation. Socrates said, "First, decide upon all the areas where you agree before moving on to more controversial areas where you have differences of opinion."

As described in a previous chapter (The Law of Four), I recommend that you start off the negotiation or discussion by going through every single item, one at a time. You'll find that there are always a large number of issues on which you and the other person agree, and which both of you accept. When you both discuss and agree on a variety of issues, you build a positive momentum toward reaching an agreement.

PUT THINGS OFF

Whenever you are going through the various issues in a negotiation and you come to a point the other person disagrees with or is adamant about, you immediately say, "Let's come back to that."

The faster you go past a controversial issue, the less negativity and resistance there will be on the part of the other person. The more items that you agree upon initially, the easier it is for the other person to agree on other items later. By making the discussion smooth and easy at the beginning, the other party will want to reciprocate by making subsequent issues smooth and easy.

At the beginning of a negotiation, be a "go-giver" rather than a go-getter. Look for every way that you can possibly agree with the other person. This way you'll build a greater and greater propensity for the other person to want to agree with you.

AGREE SLOWLY

Another negotiating tactic you can use, even if you have no problems with a particular point, is to agree to it slowly, reluctantly, and carefully. When you make a concession too quickly, without hinting at some reluctance, the other party is going to believe the matter is unimportant to you. But when you act as if a concession is important, you trigger within the other person the knowledge that he will need to reciprocate later on.

Push the Fairness Button

One of the most important emotional principles in human relationships and negotiating is the principle of fairness. Use the word *fair* as often as you can because it triggers within the mind of the other person a desire to reciprocate in a positive way. Make statements such as, "I think the fair thing to do here would be this," or "That doesn't really seem fair to me in this situation." Or, "I just want to be fair to both of us." No one will ever argue with you about your desire to be fair.

Ask the Other Party to Reciprocate

When you have reluctantly conceded on a series of minor points, you can then say, "Look, we've agreed to your requests in each of these areas. We've done all the giving up until now, and all we are asking is that you give us a little bit in these other areas"—which, of course, are the most important areas to you.

Price and Terms Are Different

Remember that price and terms are very different elements in a negotiation. You can agree to a price that may be more than you want to pay, as long as you can get terms that are favorable to you. You can tell the other party that you will pay the higher price if they will reciprocate by giving you better terms of payment.

Some friends of mine were negotiating on a million-dollar property. The property itself, based on market comparables, was not worth more than about $600,000. But the sellers demanded a million dollars for their land because a close personal friend of theirs had sold a parcel of similar size for a million dollars earlier that year. Of course, the other parcel of land was much better located, more suitable for development, and more valuable. But the owners of the land insisted that they receive $1 million for their land as well, or they wouldn't sell it at all.

My friends finally agreed to pay the asking price, as long as they could receive acceptable terms from the vendor. The terms were that they would pay the million dollars over twenty years, at $50,000 per year, with no interest. When they developed the land into separate parcels and sold the parcels, they would accelerate the payment to the vendor as they received payment from their customers.

Since the price tag of $1 million was the most important factor for the land owners, and the terms and conditions were the most important factors for my friends, they were able to enter into a satisfactory agreement where both parties got the most important thing that they wanted from the sale.

Very often, when you enter into a negotiation, it will appear at the beginning that there is no room for you to reach agreement. But when you change the focus of attention away from the price, which is usually the major issue, to the terms and conditions of the purchase, you can often find a win-win agreement that makes both parties happy. Some of the most important business deals in history have been done in this way.

SEVENTEEN

Persuasion by Social Proof

ONE OF THE most powerful influences on thinking is what other people "like me" have done in a similar situation. We are inordinately influenced by the behaviors of other people with whom we identify and to whom we relate.

Keeping Up with the Joneses

I remember a door-to-door magazine saleswoman coming to my home one day. She was friendly and cheerful. She introduced herself and then said, "I've been calling on your neighbors, and the average person I talk to subscribes to six of the magazines that I represent. I thought you might be interested in looking at this list as well."

To paraphrase the words from the movie *Jerry Maguire*, "She had me at *hello*."

Before we had a chance to think about it, we had sub-scribed to six new magazines as well. I doubt if we ever read the magazines, but what the heck, if everybody in our neighborhood was buying an average of six of these magazines, how could we refuse?

People Like Us

We are greatly influenced by what other people have done or purchased, especially people we feel are similar to us in interests, occupation, income, or even religious or political affiliation. You can be negotiating with someone and the person appears negative or uninterested. Then you say, "Well, the reason I'm talking to you is because your brother just bought two of these widgets last week." All of a sudden, the other person almost always wants to buy instantly, just in learning that someone he knows, likes, and respects has also made the same purchase or entered into the same agreement.

Gather Social Proof

Use facts, statistics, names, numbers, evidence, and proof from people known to the other party. When you use social proof, referring to others who have made the same decision, this implies that the terms and conditions you are asking for are reasonable.

For example, when you are buying a new car, the sales-person will often say, "People in business, like yourself, always choose the GPS option when they purchase this car."

Your knees go weak when the other person tells you that "people like you" have already made this buying decision and entered into this particular agreement. It knocks the chair out from under you, lowering your mental and emotional resistance.

Mention "similar others in similar situations" who have made similar decisions and concessions. When you continually refer to other people who have entered into a similar agreement, it demonstrates the reasonableness and fairness of what you are asking. It is a powerful persuader.

People in the Same Occupation

Let's say you are negotiating with a doctor to purchase a new computer and operating system to manage his practice. When you say that several other doctors in his specialty have already purchased this system, his resistance to purchasing almost disappears.

Whenever you are negotiating a particular term or condition that is controversial to the other party, give examples of other people, similar to this person, who may have resisted this term or condition initially, but eventually agreed to it. It is much easier for people to relent on a position when you tell them that other people like them have relented on this position or demand as well.

Use Testimonials of All Kinds

One of the most powerful demonstrations of social proof is when you give written testimonials, letters, or lists of other people who have entered into an agreement on the same terms and conditions that you are suggesting.

Not long ago, I was negotiating a large consulting and training contract with a major bank. Because of the cost, the decision went all the way up the line to the president. He sent back the message that he was not comfortable entering into the agreement. But if I could provide him with the names of other banks with which I had worked, he might change his mind.

Within twenty-four hours, I provided him with a list of ten banks, national and international, with whom I had worked in years past. I even gave him the names and telephone numbers of my contact people in each of the banks. However, within five minutes of seeing the list, he immediately agreed and signed the contract. He never even phoned anyone or required any proof. He just needed to know that other people "like him" had used the services that I was recommending to his bank.

By going into a negotiation prepared to give the names of individuals and organizations that have already made this buying decision, under these terms and conditions, you significantly improve your likelihood of getting a better deal. It is one of the most powerful tools for successful negotiating ever discovered.

EIGHTEEN

Price Negotiating Tactics

IN CHAPTER THREE, we talked about two types of negotiation: the short-term, onetime negotiation and the long-term business negotiation. In the short-term negotiation, your job is to get the very best price and terms at this moment, without concern for whether you will ever see or work with this person again.

There are a series of price negotiating tactics that you can use to get a better price or deal in a one-off purchase or sale. Fortunately, these tactics also work in negotiating a long-term business arrangement where you will be negotiating with the same party again, year after year.

Tactic 1: The Flinch

No matter what price the other person offers, *flinch* as if you just heard something disappointing. Put a sad or pained look on your face. Roll your eyes upward and back as though you were experiencing great pain. Say something like, "Gee! That's an awful lot of money!"

Surprisingly, sometimes just flinching will cause the other person to alter the price immediately. And if the first flinch gets you a lower price when you are buying, or a higher offer if you are selling, be prepared to use the flinch again and again throughout the negotiation.

Tactic 2: Question

Ask, "Is that the best you can do? Can't you do any better than that?"

When you ask the price and the person responds with the price, pause, look surprised or even shocked, and say, "Is that the *best* you can do?" And then remain perfectly silent. If there is any flexibility, often the other person will drop the price or otherwise raise the offer immediately.

If the person lowers the price in response to your questioning whether it's "the best you can do," you then say, "Is that the very best you can do?" Keep pressing for the lowest possible price and best terms. Follow up by again asking, "Couldn't you do any better than that?" Remember, the people you are negotiating with don't know if you've spoken to anyone else who's gotten a better deal from them.

You can also ask, "What is the best you can do if I make a decision today?" This adds an element of urgency and triggers in the mind of the vendor the fear of losing the sale.

Sometimes you can ask the question, "Are you telling me that you've never sold this item for less than that amount to anybody else? Nobody has ever bought it for less than that price?" Whenever you ask this kind of direct question, people will feel almost obligated to tell you truthfully whether they have ever sold it at a lower price.

GET IT ON SALE

In purchasing something at retail, such as furniture, appliances, or lawn equipment, you can ask, "Do you ever have this item on sale?"

Most retail organizations have special sales on certain items every year. When they tell you that this item usually goes on sale in the spring, you can then reply, "Well, I missed the sale the last time, but I would like to get it at that price today."

Sometimes, just giving sellers a good reason to give you a better price will sway them and influence them to lower the price for you.

Tactic 3: Assertion

Whatever price they give you for a particular item, you immediately reply, "I can get it cheaper somewhere else."

Whenever you tell salespeople that you can get that item cheaper from one of their competitors, they immediately soften and begin to backpedal on the price. The assertion that "I can get it cheaper elsewhere" often demolishes price resistance because the seller now thinks that you will go somewhere else.

Remember, always be friendly and genial, even in this type of negotiation. When you ask in a pleasant way, it's much easier for the person to concede to you than if you are serious or aggressive.

Tactic 4: Lowball

When someone asks you for $100, you lowball your answer and say, "I'll give you $50 cash right now."

Whenever you offer cash immediately, the price resistance of the other party diminishes dramatically. There are reasons why offering an all-cash deal causes people to be more open to doing business with you. The three most obvious ones are 1) reduced inventory costs, 2) no credit card merchant fees, and 3) the feeling of "instant gratification."

As another example, let's say you offer $50 for a $100 item and the seller comes back with an offer of $60. Very often you will find that even if you lowball at a price that seems ridiculous, sellers will still be willing to sell to you for much less than you ever thought you would have to pay.

Tactic 5: The Nibble

A nibble is an *add-on*. You say something like, "Okay, I'll agree to this price if you will throw in free delivery."

If the other party hesitates about adding something else into the deal, you can say in a pleasant way, "If you won't include free delivery, then I don't want the deal at all."

Here is the key to using the nibble. Agree on the purchase of the main item. Agree on the price and terms. Make it appear as if it is a done deal. The seller thinks he has sold the item at a price that he is happy to receive. Then you add on additional requests. It's a tactic that works even if the "item" you are buying is a house, a car, or a boat.

LESSONS FROM BUYING A HOUSE

You have just agreed to purchase a house for a certain price. Once you have agreed to the purchase price and occupancy date, but before you sign anything, you request that the sellers include the furniture, drapes, and lawn equipment in the offering price. It is quite amazing how many people will sell an entire home, as is, for the same price that they were asking for the house itself.

In the wake of the dramatic decline of the real estate market, a friend of mine purchased a house that had been offered for sale at $2.4 million. After six months of negotiation, the older couple finally agreed to a price of $1 million, just to be free of the house and the costs of maintenance. Then my friend, who is an excellent negotiator, said, "Of course, this price includes all the furniture, including the artwork, doesn't it?"

As it happened, the home was extremely well furnished and there was more than $100,000 worth of artwork inside. But because they were eager to sell the house, and also realized they had no place to put the furniture, they said, "What the heck," and gave him everything he asked for, even though they ended up selling at a dramatically lower price than they had hoped to get.

NINETEEN

The Walk-Away Method

THIS IS ONE of the most powerful tools in negotiation. In fact, you should never enter into a serious negotiation unless you are prepared to walk away if you do not achieve your most important goals in a transaction.

Previously, we talked about the importance of developing options (Chapter Twelve) and finding out what else is available. It is important to do research on your negotiating partners to find out what their real wants, needs, and problems are. When you go into a negotiation, you should have all the information you need so that you can walk away if you are not satisfied with the price or terms.

The reverse of developing options is to go into a negotiation with no choice but to find some way to agree with the other person. When you have no options, you have no choices.

When you have no choices, you have no freedom. And the more freedom you have in a negotiation, the better deal you are going to get for yourself.

Be Prepared to Walk Away from Every Negotiation

In negotiating, I do everything possible to be in a position where I can walk away at any time. It gives me tremendous bargaining strength. It almost always ensures that I get a better deal than I would have received if I had not developed my options and was not willing to "pull the trigger."

Use the walk-away method when you wish to get the lowest price possible when you are buying, and the highest price possible when you are selling. In a negotiation, I will often say, "Just tell me your very best price, one time, and I will tell you yes or no, whether I will buy it or not."

Take the Advantage

This type of statement often unnerves other people. They were expecting to start with a much different price. Now they are faced with my walking away at the very beginning if their price is unreasonable.

Or, if I'm the buyer, I will say to the seller, "You tell me what your walk-away price is." In other words, you tell me the price below which you will not sell. You tell me your final price, and if I can meet it, then we can discuss it. But if I can't, then I'll walk away and we'll forget it.

Very often, this approach gets you immediately to a price that is far below the price the other party was going to start with.

Refuse to Quibble

Especially when I'm in a hurry, I prefer not to quibble. I prefer the walk-away price. I have bought houses, cars, appliances, and many other things using the walk-away close. When I am selling something, I begin almost every conversation by saying, "This is the least amount that I will accept. If this amount is not acceptable, I understand."

Sometimes, people will ask, "What if you really want to buy the product or service, and now you have boxed yourself in by saying that you will walk away?"

Simple. Remember that walking away is merely another way of negotiating. You can get up and walk out of the room or out of the store, and then turn around and come back. But the rule is this: You never know the best price until you get up and threaten to walk away.

Lessons from Buying a Car

When I wanted to buy my wife a new car, we went to the dealership selling the kind of car she wanted. My wife and I were accompanied by two friends who are quite knowledgeable about buying and selling cars.

After viewing and trying out the car that was exactly right for my wife, we sat down for the negotiation. But first, I said, "I have worked in the car business for many years. I know exactly how much these cars are marked up, and how much profit you need to make per car to stay in business. Please tell me your very best price for this car, and I will tell you whether or not it is acceptable. Is that okay?"

The saleswoman beamed and said that would be perfectly acceptable. She then gave a price of $30,000 for a car that I knew the dealer could sell for $25,000 and still make a profit.

I looked at the number and said, "Thank you. Here is what I will do: I will pay you $25,000 in cash for this car, right now, all in, including taxes and preparation."

When she insisted that $30,000 was the best price she could offer, my wife, our two friends, and I got up and headed for the parking lot. The saleswoman ran after us and said she needed to talk to her manager. After some discussion between the two of them, the saleswoman returned with an "absolutely best" price of $28,995. Once again, we walked out.

We went back and forth like this three or four times. The saleswoman would come in, insist that she had the lowest possible price that she could give, and we would walk out. Finally, with her sales manager and other people all involved, she offered to sell the car to me for $25,000.

Remember, you never know what the best price is until you get up and walk away. You simply must develop the courage to do it, over and over, until it becomes a normal and natural part of your negotiating skills.

TWENTY

Negotiations Are Never Final

NEGOTIATION SHOULD be seen as an ongoing process. No negotiation is ever final. If you get new information that changes your perspective on the situation, go back and ask to reopen the negotiation.

We talked before about the "Chinese contract." If you are negotiating with another party with whom you intend to negotiate again and again over the years, the happiness of the other party should be an important concern of yours. Invite the other party to come back to you if the situation changes and the party is no longer happy with what you have agreed upon.

Never feel trapped after you have signed an agreement after a negotiation. Always be willing to go back and ask people to change the terms and conditions. All they can say is no, and in most cases, when it is a long-term negotiation, intelligent businesspeople will seek a way to make you happy, taking into consideration the changes in the situation that have taken place.

Offer Something in Exchange

When you go back and ask to renegotiate an agreement, be sure that you have something to offer. No one is going to seriously renegotiate an agreement with you unless it is somehow apparent that there's a benefit or advantage to them of some kind. It is your responsibility to think through what you can offer the other party before you ask the other to relent on a condition that will end up costing him money in some way.

Think through the benefit or advantage that you can offer to the other party as an incentive to reopen the negotiations and change the terms and conditions. Write out a list of all the things you have to offer, and "sell" your request to renegotiate on the basis of these benefits to the other party.

Go to Your Bank

Earlier in my business career, I ran into financial difficulties. The economy had collapsed suddenly and my business had shrunk by more than 50 percent. I had a bank loan and I could no longer make the monthly payments on that loan. What could I do?

I found out a little secret in the banking industry. If a loan goes bad, bank managers or loan officers get into serious trouble with their superiors. But you can keep a loan *current* if you simply pay the interest every month. As long as the bank is receiving the interest on the principal that it has advanced, the loan is still considered current on the bank's books and no one gets into any trouble.

So I went to my bank manager, Bob Murray, and told him that I could no longer make the monthly principal payments, but I would keep the loan current by making the interest payments if he would cut me a little slack for a few months until my business improved.

To my surprise, he agreed immediately. He rewrote the loan in front of me, calculated the amount of monthly interest on the loan, and asked me if I could make those payments each month.

I assured him that I could. He thanked me very much, shook my hand, and our relationship went on without a hiccup.

Call Your Creditors

On another occasion, my business got into serious trouble and I could no longer pay all my bills. I had thousands of dollars of accounts payable for printing, rent, utilities, shipping, recording, and legal and other business services. It is a very unpleasant situation to be in.

So, instead of avoiding the phone calls and collection agents, I made a list of all of my creditors, and then visited each one of them personally, face-to-face. I told them all the same story.

"In this economic recession, my business is in serious difficulty," I said. "But there is light at the end of the tunnel. I can see that within three to six months, my business will recover substantially, and I will be able to repay you every cent I owe you, with interest. However, if you continue to call me and insist on payment, I will simply collapse my company, put it into bankruptcy, and walk away. You will not receive a penny. What would you like to do?"

Businesspeople Are Flexible

Again, it was amazing. They said, "If you will commit to making a small payment on your account each month, this will enable us to keep your account current. In that case, we will work with you until your business turns around and you can pay it all back in full."

So I did, and they did, and we all did. Within six months, my business had recovered and I paid back every penny that I owed.

If you are currently in a bad situation because of a negotiation you entered into in the past, or because of expenses that you incurred that you cannot currently meet, don't be afraid to go back and ask for a change in terms and conditions. If you are reasonable and offer a reasonable solution, you will be amazed at how reasonable other people will be as well.

TWENTY-ONE

The Successful Negotiator

WHAT ARE the marks of a successful negotiator and how can you tell if you are one? If you observe successful negotiators, you will find several common characteristics and practices.

First, they view negotiating as a lifelong process; it is never-ending. They see all of life as a process of compromising and adjusting to conflicting interests. It goes on continuously every day, in almost every area. Ideally, it is a win-win process, but this outcome is sometimes neither desirable nor necessary.

Good negotiators are open-minded and adaptive to a changing situation. They don't adopt rigid positions. The poor negotiator gets one idea in mind and fights for it, even if the situation has changed.

Good negotiators are flexible and quick to identify mutual goals in the negotiation. They are willing to change or drop a position if new information suggests that it would be a good idea.

Successful negotiators are cooperative, not combative. They don't look upon negotiating as a fight or view themselves in an adversarial relationship.

Excellent negotiators are creative rather than competitive. Rather than just trying to win, they seek to find a solution that both parties will be happy with.

Finally, and most important, they aren't manipulative. They do not use tricks or deceit to maneuver the other party into a win-lose situation, where they win and the other person loses.

In one-off negotiating, the good negotiator does everything possible to get the very best deal, understanding that this is the only time a negotiation will take place. Whatever the terms agreed upon, the two parties will probably never negotiate again. The goal is to get the best deal.

However, in business negotiating, where the two parties will probably negotiate and work together again, the excellent negotiator is already thinking about the next negotiation before the current negotiation has been finalized. The negotiator's thinking must be long term.

In all my years of negotiating, I have never found that smart negotiators enter into superior deals as the result of any kind of trickery. There are many books and courses that tell you how to use tactics like "role reversals" and "good guy/bad guy" techniques, where you try to trick people psychologically into making commitments or decisions. These methods seldom work in the real world.

In the real world, it is honest, straightforward, direct, sincere men and women with a clear idea of what they want to accomplish, and a commitment to entering into an agreement that everybody can live with, who are the most successful in negotiating.

You do not have to be cunning and manipulative to be successful as a negotiator. You can instead be straightforward, honest, and completely clear about what you want, and then seek the best way to get it in your discussion with the other party.

The Four Essentials

Remember the four essentials of negotiating upon which all successful negotiations are based. If you remember these four keys, you will become and remain an excellent negotiator:

1. *Get the facts and prepare in advance.* The power is always on the side of the person with the most knowledge, the most options, the most information, and the best alternatives. Prepare in advance, and learn everything you possibly can about the wants, needs, and the situation of the other party.

2. *Ask for what you want.* Ask your way to success. Say, "Before we begin, I would like to tell you what

I would really like to come out of this negotiation with." Don't be afraid to ask for a lot when going into a negotiation, especially on price and terms, because these are always arbitrary elements that are subject to discussion and change.

3. *Seek win-win solutions.* In any long-term ongoing business arrangement, do not try to win or manipulate to get an agreement that is to the disadvantage of the other party. Seek a win-win or no deal. Remember that life is long, and what goes around comes around. If you enter into an agreement that is harmful to the other person today, it can come back to haunt you later on in your career and cost far more than the short-term advantage that you gained.

4. *Practice, practice, practice.* Negotiate on every occasion and at every opportunity. Whether you are buying clothes, cars, appliances, or property, be sure to practice, practice, practice your negotiation skills. Your ability to negotiate, which only comes with continual practice, can save you 20 percent or more of everything you earn or spend for the rest of your life. Good negotiating skills can save you money, time, and energy. They can make you a much more effective person and contribute substantially to the success of your career in business and in life.

Good negotiators are made, not born. The good news is that you can learn to be an excellent negotiator by studying the subject, by applying what you have learned in this book, and by practicing these techniques over and over again until they become second nature. You'll have ample opportunity because negotiation is a lifelong process. It never ends.

Good luck!

INDEX

ABOUT THE AUTHOR

Brian Tracy is a professional speaker, trainer, seminar leader, and consultant, and chairman of Brian Tracy International, a training and consulting company based in Solana Beach, California.

Brian bootstrapped his way to success. In 1981, in talks and seminars around the U.S., he began teaching the principles he forged in sales and business. Today, his books and audio and video programs—more than 500 of them—are available in 38 languages and are used in 55 countries.

He is the bestselling author of more than fifty books, including *Full Engagement* and *Reinvention*.

"Inspiring, entertaining, informative, motivational..."

Brian Tracy is one of the world's top speakers. He addresses more than 250,000 people annually—in over 100 appearances—and has consulted and trained at more than 1,000 corporations. In his career he has reached over five million people in 58 countries. He has lived and practiced every principle in his writing and speeches:

21st-Century Thinking: How to outmaneuver the competition and get superior results in an ever-turbulent business climate.

Leadership in the New Millennium: Learn the most powerful leadership principles—ever—to get maximum results, faster.

Advanced Selling Strategies: How to use modern sales' most advanced strategies and tactics to outperform your competitors.

The Psychology of Success: Think and act like the top performers. Learn practical, proven techniques for excellence.

To book Brian to speak at your next meeting or conference, visit Brian Tracy International at www.briantracy.com, or call (858) 436-7316 for a free promotional package. Brian will carefully customize his talk to your specific needs.

Other titles by Brian Tracy available in ebook format:

The Brian Tracy Success Library:
 Motivation ISBN: 978-08144-33126

The Brian Tracy Success Library:
 Delegation & Supervision ISBN: 978-08144-33157

The Brian Tracy Success Library:
 Negotiation ISBN: 978-08144-33195

Crunch Point ISBN: 978-08144-30132

Focal Point ISBN: 9780-8144-26258

Full Engagement ISBN: 978-08144-16907

How the Best Leaders Lead ISBN: 978-08144-14354

Now, Build a Great Business ISBN: 978-08144-16983

The Power of Charm ISBN: 978-08144-29716

Reinvention ISBN: 978-08144-13470

Speak to Win ISBN: 978-08144-01828

Time Power ISBN: 978-08144-27859

TurboStrategy ISBN: 978-08144-29303

For more information, please visit: www.amacombooks.org

To learn more about Brian Tracy visit his website: http://www.briantracy.com/

About AMACOM

Who We Are: AMACOM is the book publishing division of the American Management Association (www.amanet.org). AMACOM's broad range of offerings spans not only the critical business topics and leadership challenges of today and tomorrow, but also the issues that affect our lives, our work, and our world.

What We Publish: AMACOM publishes non-fiction books on business, management, leadership, HR, training, communications, career growth, personal development, marketing, sales, customer service, project management and finance.

About Our Authors: AMACOM authors are experts in their fields, unrivaled in their knowledge, experience, and reputation. They are world-class educators, successful executives, business owners, trainers, consultants, and journalists—all eager to share their insights and techniques with a broad audience.